D0893394

SNAPSHOTS IN HISTORY

THE HUNDRED DAYS OFFENSIVE

The Allies' Push to Win World War I

by Andrew Langley

SNAPSHOTS IN HISTORY

THE HUNDRED DAYS OFFENSIVE

The Allies' Push to Win World War I

by Andrew Langley

Content Adviser: Tom Lansford, Ph.D.,
Assistant Dean and Associate Professor of Political Science,
College of Arts and Letters,
University of Southern Mississippi

Reading Adviser: Susan Kesselring, M.A., Literacy Educator,
Rosemount-Apple Valley-Eagan (Minnesota) School District

Compass Point Books ✦ Minneapolis, Minnesota

Compass Point Books

151 Good Counsel Drive
P.O. Box 669
Mankato, MN 56002–0669

 This book was manufactured with paper containing
at least 10 percent post-consumer waste.

For Compass Point Books
Brenda Haugen, XNR Productions, Inc., Catherine Neitge,
Keith Griffin, Ashlee Suker, LuAnn Ascheman-Adams, and Nick Healy

Produced by White-Thomson Publishing Ltd.
For White-Thomson Publishing
Stephen White-Thomson, Susan Crean, Amy Sparks,
Clare Nicholas, Peggy Bresnick Kendler, and Timothy Griffin

Library of Congress Cataloging-in-Publication Data
Langley, Andrew.
The hundred days offensive : the Allies' push to win World War I / by
Andrew Langley.
   p. cm. — (Snapshots in history)
 Includes bibliographical references and index.
 ISBN 978-0-7565-3858-3 (library binding)
1. World War, 1914–1918—Campaigns—Western Front—Juvenile
literature. 2. World War, 1914–1918—Campaigns—France—Juvenile
literature. I. Title. II. Series.
 D530.L36 2008
 940.4'34—dc22   2008007543

Visit Compass Point Books on the Internet at
www.compasspointbooks.com
or e-mail your request to
custserv@compasspointbooks.com

CONTENTS

Breaking Through

Just before dawn on August 8, 1918, fog spread across the low-lying French countryside near the town of Amiens, not far from France's border with Belgium. It gave cover to waves of soldiers as they moved quietly into position. Within a few hours many thousands of Allied troops— British, French, Australian, and Canadian—were stationed on a line that stretched for 15 miles (24 kilometers).

Fresh and eager infantry regiments from the United States stood alongside their tired Allies. It was the first time many American soldiers would enter combat, and they approached the coming battle with a refreshing energy. Behind them, more than 500 tanks and 2,000 field guns stood ready for action.

The Allies had been fighting World War I for four years. Neither they nor their enemy had been able to gain the upper hand, and the two sides were stuck in a deadlock along the Western Front. An Australian soldier, J.R. Armitage, described the scene on that fateful morning near Ameins, which marked the beginning of the end of the long, deadly war.

It was utterly still. Vehicles made no sound on the marshy ground. ... The silence played on our nerves a bit. As we got our guns into position you could hear drivers whispering to their horses and men muttering curses under their breath.

British troops advanced in the shadow of tanks fitted with special equipment for the battle conditions.

9

Somewhere in the darkness ahead was the enemy—the German army—unaware that a major attack was about to begin. At 4:20 A.M. the roar of Allied artillery shattered the silence. The Battle of Amiens had begun.

Shells screamed overhead crashing down only 200 yards (182 meters) in front of the Allied soldiers. The noise was deafening. Armitage recalled, "The world was enveloped in sound and flame. The ground shook."

Two minutes later, Allied gunners altered their aim, and the shells landed farther behind enemy lines. The rain of explosives and flying metal swept forward, covering all enemy positions. This moving barrage, creeping slowly ahead, left room for the Allied forces to advance in safety.

All along the front line, Allied soldiers surged forward in what would become the Hundred Days Offensive, the final Allied offensive in World War I. First went the tanks, clanking loudly over the ground at a walking pace. Armed with cannons or machine guns at the sides, the tanks were a reliable way to advance through mud, barbed wire, and bullets. They left wide gaps in the German defenses by smashing holes in the barbed wire and crushing machine-gun posts meant to protect the enemy. The tanks also tore up telephone cables, leaving the enemy's front line troops unable to communicate with their command centers in the rear.

The tanks terrified the Germans, but the men inside them also suffered. British Captain Gordon Hassell commanded a tank at the Battle of Amiens. He described what it was like for the tank operators:

> *Noisy, hot, airless and bumpy. One caught at a handhold, and got a burn on the hot engine. … If the tank was hit slivers of hot steel began to fly—bullets hitting the armored plates caused melting and the splash was dangerous to the eyes.*

The Allies used German prisoners to carry wounded Allied troops from the battleground.

Behind the tanks came the first wave of Canadian and Australian soldiers. They stormed through the gaps in the barbed wire, leaped into the trenches where the enemy was hidden, and killed or captured everyone in sight. Then they moved on to the next set of trenches.

The sudden and terrifying assault took the Germans by surprise. They could see very little in the darkness and the fog. All they could hear was the thunder of the barrage and the rumble of the tanks. They were so confused that they did not open fire for five minutes after the attack began. Even then, their machine-gun bullets bounced harmlessly off the tank armor.

LIFE IN THE TRENCHES

A trench was about 8 feet (2.4 meters) deep. The soldiers slept and took shelter from gunfire in dugout holes on either side. On the front side of the trench was a ridge called a firestep, where soldiers stood to shoot at the enemy. Drainage was a big problem. In winter, water in the trenches soon turned to mud, which could be more than 3 feet (90 cm) deep.

The Allied troops, armored cars, and tanks quickly forced their way into territory held by the Germans. By 8 A.M. they had gained more than 4,000 yards (3,640 m) of ground. Then a second wave of soldiers arrived to push even farther ahead. The advance continued. By midmorning, the Australians had moved so far that they reached the rear of the enemy lines.

Germany had been at war for more than four years. Its troops were struggling and tired. When the Allies attacked at Amiens, huge numbers of Germans simply gave up, throwing down their weapons and surrendering. Many others fled eastward in panic, chased by the Allied armored cars firing their mounted machine guns. The Germans had no time to get together and make a stand that would delay the attackers.

But it was not all easy going for the Allies. British and American troops in the northern part of the battle had fewer tanks to lead the way. They also had to cross over broken ground, go through dense

Thousands of German prisoners captured in the Battle of Amiens waited to see where they would be imprisoned.

13

woodland, and then capture a ridge. The Germans here fought hard and forced the British and Americans to halt before reaching their target.

Even so, the opening day of the four-day Battle of Amiens was a stunning success. In a single day, Allied forces tore a huge hole in the front line, which had stood firm for more than three years. In places, they pushed the German army back more than 7 miles (11.2 km). Altogether, they captured more than 100 square miles (260 square kilometers) of enemy territory. Nearly 30,000 German soldiers were killed, captured, or wounded.

THE TWO SIDES IN WORLD WAR I

Key Allied Powers:
Australia
Belgium
Canada
France (including the colonies
    of Algeria and Morocco)
Great Britain
Greece
India
Italy
New Zealand
Russia (until November 1917)
Serbia
South Africa
United States (entered the
    war in April 1917)

Central Powers:
Austria-Hungary (an empire
    that included most of
    Central Europe)
Bulgaria
Germany
Ottoman Empire (which
    included Turkey, most of
    Southeast Europe, and
    parts of the Middle East
    and North Africa)

German leaders knew that the Battle of Amiens would become a turning point in the war. It was clear that many of their troops had lost heart. General Erich Ludendorff, commander of the German army, was shocked by their behavior. He later wrote:

> *August 8 was the Black Day of the German Army. It put the decline of our fighting powers beyond all doubt. Whole bodies of our men had surrendered to single troopers or isolated squadrons. The officers had lost their influence. Our war machine was no longer efficient.*

The speed of the advance amazed the Allies—even the officers who had planned it. But not one of the officers could be sure that their attack would succeed completely. Final victory seemed a long way off. ◣

The World at War

2

A half-century before World War I started, a new force arose in global affairs—nationalism. Small countries united into larger blocs, and these large blocs became nations. People felt a growing loyalty to their nation. They became determined that it should be bigger and stronger than others.

Some nations, such as Great Britain, Germany, and Russia, had grown more powerful than others. The stronger they grew, the more they came into conflict with one another over territory, trade, and military power. Fear and suspicion arose from this rivalry. As a result, nations looked for allies that would support them if they were attacked. They also began to build up their armed forces and develop new and more deadly weapons.

In the years leading up to war, Germany built up a powerful fleet of battleships.

By 1914, much of Europe was divided into two sides that had grown increasingly hostile toward each other. On one side were the Central Powers, which were led by Germany and the empire of Austria-Hungary. On the other side were the Allies, led by Great Britain, France, and Russia.

That year, an assassination led to the start of World War I. The victim was Archduke Franz Ferdinand, heir to the throne of Austria-Hungary. On June 28, 1914, he and his wife, Sophie, were shot and killed while visiting the town of Sarajevo in Bosnia and Herzegovina. Their murderer was caught immediately, and Austrian leaders claimed that he belonged to a terrorist group from nearby Serbia.

Alliances between the various nations triggered the series of war declarations that followed. This led to the biggest war the world had ever seen. About 15 million people died, although the exact number of deaths that resulted from the war will never be known.

On July 28, 1914, exactly one month after the assassinations, Austria-Hungary declared war on Serbia. Russia, as an ally of Serbia, began moving its vast armies to the borders of Germany and Austria-Hungary. On August 1, Germany declared war on Russia. Two days later, Germany also declared war on France, Russia's closest ally.

A German invasion force advanced into France, passing through Belgium on the way. Because

Archduke Franz Ferdinand was heir to the throne of Austria-Hungary, an empire that stretched from Austria to Poland and parts of Italy. He and his wife, Sophie, were shot and killed in Sarajevo, in Bosnia and Herzegovina.

the British government had promised to protect Belgium, Great Britain declared war on Germany on August 4, 1914. With it came the support of troops from all parts of the huge British Empire, including Australia, Canada, New Zealand, and India.

At this stage, the United States remained neutral in the war. Most Americans did not want to be involved in a war in Europe.

The French, Belgian, and British armies had become the major nations of the side known as the Allies. They were fighting against the Central Powers, led by Germany and Austria-Hungary. One of the main areas of conflict between the two sides was in northern France. By late November, the Allies had brought the Germans to a complete stop on a line stretching more than 450 miles (720 km) between the North Sea coast and the Swiss border. This line became known as the Western Front.

The Western Front divided Europe during World War I.

The Western Front, 1915

Along the Western Front, the Germans reached a lasting deadlock against the British, French, and Belgians. On each side of the line, soldiers strung barriers of barbed wire, and behind these they dug systems of trenches to give them shelter from enemy bullets. The trenches were often deep and filled with mud or water. They also often served as home to rats and lice. There the troops lived, fired at the enemy, and occasionally launched attacks.

Assaulting the enemy from this position was difficult. First the soldiers had to climb up out of their trenches. This was called "going over the top." Then they had to advance across no-man's land, the gap between the two sides, somehow scrambling past huge shell holes and tangles of wire. Out in the open, they faced the deadly fire of rifles and machine guns from enemy trenches. But these assaults usually failed, with a shockingly heavy death toll.

THE EASTERN FRONT

Germany and Austria-Hungary fought along their eastern borders as well as on the Western Front. In August 1914, the Russians attacked Germany from the east. The Germans forced them to retreat, but the conflict took away valuable troops from the fighting in France. Austria-Hungary faced another enemy—Italy, which entered the war on the Allied side in 1915. The two sides fought a long battle in the rugged mountains of the Alps. In 1916, Austria-Hungary also faced a fresh attack from Russia. The conflict left the armies of both countries exhausted and short of soldiers and weapons.

New weapons such as machine guns, poison gas, and high-explosive shells had created a kind of warfare not seen before. Pinned down in their trenches, armies were unable to move. From behind the lines, the big guns of the artillery sent barrages of shells overhead, which deafened the soldiers and turned the landscape into a sea of mud and craters.

Edwin Vaughan, a young British officer, described the terrible scene after a trench battle, as the noise of the guns faded away:

Poison Gas

The Germans first used chlorine gas as a weapon in April 1915 in France. Released from cylinders, the gas drifted across to the enemy lines. Those who inhaled it felt a burning in their throats and eyes. The British and French used gas for the first time a few months later. By 1917, Germany had developed the more deadly "mustard" gas, which was fired in gun shells. This caused blistering of the skin and lungs, along with internal bleeding. More than 1 million soldiers died of the effects of poison gas during the war.

A more terrible sound now reached my ears. From the darkness on all sides came the groans and wails of wounded men: faint, long, sobbing moans of agony, and despairing shrieks. It was too horribly obvious that dozens of men with serious wounds must have crawled for safety into new shell-holes, and now the water was rising about them and, powerless to move, they were slowly drowning. And we could do nothing to help them.

Commanders on both sides believed that the only way to break the deadlock along the Western Front was to launch a giant offensive that would smash the opposition out of the way. Early in 1916, the Germans attacked the French city of Verdun, beginning with a massive bombardment from 1,220 guns. They failed to capture the city, although the battle lasted 10 months. Each side lost more than 100,000 men.

That summer, the Allies launched a major attack on the German lines near the River Somme. This time, the Allies failed to break through, and the battle dragged on for many months. The death toll was even more horrifying—146,000 Allies and 164,000 Germans were killed—making it one of the bloodiest battles in world history. Despite this, the Somme offensive gained little territory for the Allies.

Canadian soldiers went over the top during the Somme offensive.

Major offensives on both sides failed, and by the winter of 1916–1917 the war had turned into a never-ending torment. Millions had died or been badly wounded. Soldiers on both sides were miserable and exhausted. In the trenches, they lived in constant terror, amid disease and mud. They often went short of food, and what they did eat was of poor quality. Many who escaped death or injury suffered from a severe mental breakdown called "shell shock," which was caused by the horrors of battle.

Before the Somme attack in 1916, Allied guns had shelled the German lines for eight days.

By 1917, both the Allies and the Central Powers had lost so many men that their armies were badly weakened. The Germans realized that they did not have enough troops to make

a successful attack on the Allies. They decided to rely on strong defenses instead. They built a new line of fortifications that was much stronger than the usual trench system. The British called this the Hindenburg Line. They named it after the chief of the German army, Paul von Hindenburg.

Allied commanders still believed that the only way to win the war was through a big offensive. During 1917, there were two more massive assaults on the German front lines. The French attacked near the River Aisne, and the British and Canadians struck farther north at Passchendaele. Both attacks were disasters, costing thousands of lives and gaining little ground. It seemed that nothing would break the long deadlock along the Western Front.

While the European Allies faced gloom and failure in France, the Germans were also on the offensive elsewhere—against the United States, which was still neutral. German submarines patrolled the eastern Atlantic attacking cargo ships. The aim was to prevent vital supplies, including food and material for weapons, from reaching Great Britain. German submarines sank many American ships, causing outrage in the United States.

Also in 1917, German agents urged Mexico to invade the United States. A year earlier, U.S. troops had entered Mexico to hunt for Pancho Villa, a bandit and freedom fighter. The action angered the Mexican government. Early in 1917, a German government minister named Arthur Zimmermann sent a telegram to the German Embassy in Mexico. In his message, Zimmermann suggested trying to urge the Mexicans to gain revenge by becoming allied with Germany and invading Texas. The telegram was intercepted and published by the U.S. government, helping to turn American public opinion against Germany.

On April 2, 1917, President Woodrow Wilson called for the United States to go to war against Germany. He said:

Room 40

At the start of World War I, the British government set up an intelligence unit in London. Called Room 40 (after its office number), the unit intercepted German telegrams and other types of messages. These were usually in code, which Room 40 officers had to figure out and translate. The unit's greatest triumph was to intercept and decode the telegram from Arthur Zimmermann, which it then passed on to the U.S. government.

> *The right is more precious than peace, and we shall fight for the things which we have always carried nearest our hearts—for democracy, for the rights and liberties of small nations, for a universal dominion of right as shall bring peace and safety to all nations.*

On April 6, Congress declared war on Germany, and the United States officially joined World War I.

This was a great boost to the Allied cause, although most of the American forces would not reach the Western Front for more than a year. The U.S. Army, with 120,000 men, was still small, and many more troops would have to be recruited and trained. More equipment was desperately needed. The Army had few machine guns and no heavy artillery. Military commanders believed that the U.S. Army would not be ready for a major action until 1919. ◣

Newspaper headlines proclaimed the long-awaited entry into the war by the United States.

The Kaiser's Battle

3

The year 1917 ended with a final blow for the Allied side. Russia had the biggest army in the war, but it had suffered more than 9 million casualties during the fighting. These terrible losses, in addition to widespread poverty and food shortages at home, led to a revolution in Russia. Popular uprisings swept away the power of the tsar, or emperor, and then the Russian government. The country was in chaos, and its new leaders immediately withdrew Russia's troops from the war.

As a result, all fighting stopped on the Eastern Front. This allowed Germany to move troops from there to strengthen forces in France. By early 1918, German soldiers outnumbered Allied soldiers on the Western Front.

Russian soldiers left the front lines to listen to revolutionary leaders speak in October 1917, during the Russian Revolution.

Among the German leaders was General Erich Ludendorff. He believed that Germany had a strong chance of winning the war. But the Germans had to act quickly. The first American soldiers had already landed in France, under the command of General John J. Pershing. However, they would not be able to take part fully in the fighting for some months because they were short of equipment and battle training. The Germans had time to launch one last big offensive before the Americans were fully prepared to fight.

Ludendorff planned the operation with great care. He moved extra divisions of troops to the front line at night so that the Allies would not see them. He studied the mistakes of previous attacks and decided to use fresh tactics, such as forming a new force of "storm troopers" chosen from the fittest and best soldiers. They would lead the ground attack, carrying flame-throwers, grenades, and light machine guns, and head for the weakest points in the Allied lines.

Ludendorff invited Germany's emperor, Kaiser Wilhelm II, to visit the front line. He sent messages to German newspapers saying that Wilhelm was personally leading the offensive. It soon became known as the "Kaiser's Battle."

The attack began on March 21, 1918. About 6,000 German guns opened fire along a 40-mile (64-km) stretch near the River Somme. The Allies had the fewest soldiers on this part of the Western Front.

The mighty barrage continued for more than four hours, and then the storm troopers charged across no man's land. They moved in groups, rather than a long line, and this made them difficult to defend against. Behind them came two more waves of support troops.

Kaiser Wilhelm II inspected German troops before the March 1918 offensive.

The assault wiped out the British troops at the front of the line. One of the few who survived was Rifleman E. Chapman. He described the attack:

> *The bombardment on our trenches was sheer hell—shells, trench mortars, the lot, gradually cutting down our platoon [squad of soldiers]. While we were discussing what to do, my pal was hit with a piece of shell, which sliced his head completely off. You can imagine how I felt. All the rest were dead by now, so I decided to go along the trenches to see if I could find anybody alive.*

31

The shelling and the storm trooper attack smashed the Allied front line. The survivors had to fall back, and the German advance went on. British troops were forced to retreat 40 miles (64 km) in some places. The Germans were now very close to the important town of Amiens, which had vital rail links to the north and east that would make it easier for the Germans to move men and supplies.

More than 21,000 British soldiers were taken prisoner on March 21. It was a terrifying experience to come face-to-face with the enemy. Private Jack Rogers thought he was going to die:

> We all just threw down our guns and saw these blinkin' Prussian [German] Guards come tearing down the trench. I saw one guard coming straight for me, fixed bayonet. He came rushing up and from that moment I said goodbye—there was to be no more of me. I expected the bayonet to go directly into me but it didn't. He stopped, stood his gun down, looked at me and said "Zigaretten, Kamerad? [Cigarette, comrade?]" I nearly dropped to the ground in surprise.

Allied commanders realized that the war might be lost in the next few days and that they had to take action. On March 26, the leaders of the British and French armies appointed French Marshal Ferdinand Foch as supreme commander of all Allied forces. Foch ordered that the retreat should stop and that his troops should hold on to their present positions. To help

with this plan, reinforcements arrived from Great Britain, as well as from other parts of the Western Front.

The German offensive was already slowing down. Although the Germans had broken through the Allied line at its weakest point, other parts of the line were defended by British and French troops. On March 28, the Allies beat back a German attack, and the Germans suffered heavy losses. Despite the dramatic success of the first few days, Ludendorff knew that his great plan had failed to end the war. His army was exhausted, and German casualties were as numerous as Allied losses.

The Germans launched a second offensive farther north, in Belgium. It was yet another bitter

British soldiers captured during the 1918 Kaiser's Battle collapsed, exhausted, on a road as they traveled to prison camps inside Germany.

33

ALLIED COMMANDERS

Australia:

General John Monash

A civil engineer before the war, Monash rose to become commander of the Australian Corps in 1918. He pioneered the use of troops in coordination with tanks, artillery, and aircraft.

Belgium:

King Albert I of Belgium

King Albert became a national hero for resisting the German advance through his country in 1914.

Canada:

General Arthur Currie

Currie led the Canadian Corps through much of the war. He was a careful and cunning planner and was determined to keep the Canadians as an independent fighting force.

France:

Marshal Ferdinand Foch

In 1914, Foch led the French army, which halted the first German advance at the River Marne in 1918. As Allied supreme commander, he believed in fighting defensively until the enemy was exhausted.

Marshal Philippe Petain

Petain became famous for leading the French forces in the defense of Verdun in 1916. Starting in 1918, he was second-in-command to Foch.

Great Britain:

Field Marshal Sir Douglas Haig

Haig became commander-in-chief of British forces on the Western Front in 1915. He planned the disastrous offensives on the Somme in 1916 and Passchaendale in 1917.

United States:

General John Pershing

Strict and tough, Pershing came to Europe with the first group of U.S. troops in 1917. He was determined to keep all U.S. forces under his own control and would not allow his units to be used to reinforce other Allied armies.

The top Allied commanders included (from left): Marshal Philippe Petain, Field Marshal Sir Douglas Haig, Marshal Ferdinand Foch, and General John Pershing.

and bloody conflict, but the British defenders on this part of the line fought stubbornly and stopped the Germans from gaining ground. The British commander, Douglas Haig, told his troops, "Victory will belong to the side that holds out longest. Every position must be held to the last man."

In May and June 1918, Germany made two more large-scale attacks, this time on the French lines near the River Marne. At about the same time, U.S. forces under General John Pershing played a large part in the fighting for the first time. On May 28, American soldiers captured the town of Cantigny on the River Somme. On June 1, they helped reinforce hard-pressed French troops at Chateau-Thierry, and on June 6, they drove back a German attack at Belleau Wood.

The buildup of U.S. troops in France during 1918 boosted the confidence and manpower of the Allies.

These actions were small in scale, but the appearance of U.S. soldiers in battle was important. Unlike the European Allies, American soldiers were fresh and confident. Vera Brittain, a British nurse, described her first sight of American troops:

> *I pressed forward to watch the United States physically entering the War, so god-like, so magnificent, so unimpaired [undamaged] in comparison with the tired, nerve-racked men of the British Army.*

By July 1918, Germany was in charge of a bigger area of territory than ever before during the war. German troops were just 40 miles (64 km) from

Paris, and their biggest guns could send shells into the French capital city. But the German army had run out of strength and resources. During the Kaiser's Battle, more than 800,000 men were lost. There were not enough soldiers to replace those who had been killed, wounded, or captured.

This became clear on July 15 when the Germans crossed the River Marne. Three days later, French and U.S. forces counterattacked. They slowly pushed back the Germans, causing nearly 170,000 more casualties and taking 30,000 prisoners. By August 5, Ludendorff was forced to withdraw his forces. The Germans had lost the Battle of the Marne. For the Allies, it was a turning point. ◣

37

The Hundred Days Begin

Chapter

4

While the Battle of the Marne was still raging, Allied Supreme Commander Marshal Foch was planning the Allies' next move. On July 24, 1918, he told a meeting of the Allied chief commanders that the time had come to give up defense and go on the attack. But this would not be an all-out offensive like the disastrous assault at the River Somme in 1916. Instead, it would be a series of smaller attacks on different targets as part of a grand assault.

The first of these was near Amiens. German forces were less than 10 miles (16 km) from the town, an important junction for main roads and railways. The German line was weak there. It was not straight but bulged forward in a salient—an area that sticks out. This meant that the line was longer, so its defenders had to spread out.

German troops fought desperately as they were pushed back during the Allied offensives of September 1918.

SALIENTS

A salient is a military position that sticks out into enemy territory. Salients are often created when troops attack along a wide front. Some units are held up, while others advance more quickly. This causes a bulge in the line, something that happened frequently on the Western Front. A salient is difficult to defend, because the enemy can attack from two or three sides at once. Worse still, enemy soldiers may succeed in surrounding the salient and cutting it off from the rest of the line.

Preparations for the attack began at once. It would be the start of the final period of the war, which would come to be called the "Hundred Days Offensive." The Allies wanted to keep the plans as secret as possible. The Germans were to be taken by surprise and have no time to bring

up extra soldiers. Canadian and Australian troops were stationed well away from the front line, to the west of Amiens. Guns, wagons, and other equipment arrived at night so the enemy would not see them. The roads near the front were covered with straw to deaden the sound of the wheels so the enemy could not hear them.

Allied commanders knew that tanks would play a vital part in the offensive. More than 500 tanks were driven into position near the line on August 6 and 7. The noise of their engines and clanking wheels and tracks was loud. To drown out the sound, aircraft of Great Britain's Royal Air Force kept their own engines running. Fighter aircraft also patrolled the skies to keep enemy spotter planes away from the target area.

Some Americans were trained to use French tanks, which were faster and more mobile than British tanks.

41

Allied soldiers were told little. Officers gave them all a list of orders that said, "Keep Your Mouth Shut!" It went on to say:

> When you know that your unit is making preparations for an attack, don't talk about them to men in other units, or to strangers. If you see or hear anything, keep it to yourself.

When the Battle of Amiens began on the morning of August 8, 1918, the secret preparations paid off. The suddenness and power of the attack surprised the Germans and helped the Allied forces smash their way through the front line. The official German account of the day noted that it had

Allied troops assembling for the attack at Amiens were ordered to say nothing about the preparations.

NO WAR TALK!
Attorney General Gregory, says:
"OBEY THE LAW
Keep Your Mouth Shut!"

been "the greatest defeat which the German army had suffered since the beginning of the war." No one knew then that in 100 days the entire war would be over.

The speed of the advance caused problems the next day. The attacking forces had captured so much territory that they had run far ahead of their supplies and artillery. Now they had to wait several hours for the others to catch up. The roads were choked. Long columns of wounded men and German prisoners headed west, while fresh infantry units and ammunition wagons moved eastward.

WAR IN THE AIR

In 1914, powered aircraft were still in their early stages. At first they were used to watch enemy movements below. Then pilots started fighting each other. They began by throwing bricks and even pieces of rope at each other and then by shooting pistols or rifles. By 1915, planes were carrying machine guns. Air battles took place between bands of fighter aircraft. By the end of the war, the French, British, Italians, and Germans had developed large bomber aircraft. The British Royal Air Force was formed in April 1918, indicating the growing importance of the airplane in war.

The advance of the Allies slowed as their tank force became weaker. By the morning of August 9, only 145 of the original 500 tanks were still in operation. The others had broken down or been damaged. When the Allies reached the old 1916 battleground of the Somme, they found it pitted with trenches and shell craters, and forces had to move slowly over the terrain. At the same time, the Germans brought up reinforcements to strengthen their lines and were putting up a more determined fight.

43

That day, the Allies only gained about 3 miles (4.8 km) of enemy territory. On August 10, they moved less than half a mile (0.8 km). On the evening of August 11, the British offensive halted. Allied Commander Foch had wanted to carry on with the attack, but British Field Marshal Haig refused because he knew it would be a waste of lives. The Germans had started to withdraw their troops from the salient and move back to the Hindenburg Line. The Battle of Amiens had gained more than 12 miles (19.2 km) of ground in places, but now it was time to plan for attacks in other areas.

THE HINDENBURG LINE

The Germans began building the Hindenburg Line in 1916. This huge defense system covered nearly 100 miles (160 km) of the Western Front. It was a series of strongholds linked by deep, wide trenches and tunnels and protected by thick belts of barbed wire. Each stronghold held bunkers, which are protected defensive positions, and machine-gun nests made of concrete. As the Germans withdrew to the Hindenburg Line, they flattened everything in front of it so that attackers would have no cover. The Germans believed that the Hindenburg Line was so strong that no army would ever get past it.

After four years of failure and terrible bloodshed, the Allies at last enjoyed a victory. The advance at Amiens gave them new confidence and hope. The Germans, on the other hand, were now in despair. They were running out of experienced soldiers and had to call up teenagers with little training. The Battle of Amiens was not a final defeat, but many German military leaders felt their army would

The German army was weakened by the loss of huge numbers of soldiers captured at Amiens.

not recover from it. That evening, Kaiser Wilhelm declared, "We have nearly reached the limit of our powers of resistance. The war must be ended."

Haig now prepared for the next attacks in the grand assault. British, New Zealander, Australian, and American troops were to take the towns of Albert and Bapaume, farther north. The early morning of August 21 was foggy as the attack began. The artillery opened up with another "creeping barrage" of shells that moved ahead of the soldiers and tanks.

45

This time, however, there was no dramatic advance. Allied tanks found it difficult to make their way over the pitted ground in the looming fog. When the sun came out, it grew so hot inside the heavy tanks that many of the crew fainted. Some soldiers had to wade through mud and water from the flooded river. It was an exhausting day, but the Allies pushed the German line back by 2 miles (3.2 km).

The next day the Allied advance stopped. The Germans made a counterattack but were forced to retreat. This allowed time for another Allied army to slip past on the south side and capture the town of Albert. On August 23, both parts of the Allied attacking force came together to push forward on a massive front 35 miles (56 km) long.

WAR WEAPONS

Rifle: A trained soldier could fire between eight and 12 rifle rounds of ammunition per minute. Rifles could kill at one mile (1.6 km) but were only accurate at half that distance. A bayonet (blade) could be fitted to the end of a rifle for hand-to-hand fighting.

Machine gun: Machine guns fired rapidly and repeatedly. At the beginning of the war, machine guns weighed more than 120 pounds (54 kilograms). Crews of four to six men were needed to lift and operate them. By 1918, there were much lighter machine guns that could be used by one man.

Grenade: A grenade is a bomb thrown by hand. A soldier would pull out the safety pin and throw the grenade, which exploded four seconds later.

Mortar: Mortars were simple guns that fired small bombs. They worked well in trenches because they fired at a steep angle and had a range of 1,200 yards (1,092 m). A trained soldier could launch 22 bombs per minute.

Haig's plan was working. The Germans were falling back while still losing thousands of men every day. In the north, Canadian troops had already reached the Hindenburg Line and could go no farther until the rest of their front line caught up. By August 29, British forces passed Bapaume on both sides. The Germans retreated in a hurry, leaving the town empty for the men of the New Zealand division to move between the British forces.

Supply vehicles and support personnel followed the Allied troops as they advanced. As support moved forward, traffic became more congested.

47

The German army was running short of fit men to fight on the Western Front. German officer Friedrich Meisel was on the front line when a new bunch of recruits arrived from Germany at the end of August. He described what he saw:

> *Half of them were boys who appeared to be hardly 16; others, old men who looked quite sick. The new men told us that the present male population of Germany consisted only of cripples, deserters, and war profiteers; the people were starving, and even the babies underfed.*

Germany was by now in a desperate situation. At home, supplies of food were running out because of a sea blockade by the British navy. Royal Navy warships had blockaded German ports on the North Sea and the Baltic Sea. This action strangled the supply of food to Germany, causing great hardship for its people. The blockade also kept out the vital raw materials needed for weapons and did major damage to the German war effort.

THE CANADIANS AND VIMY RIDGE

The Canadian army's capture of Vimy Ridge near Arras in 1917 is one of the most famous actions of World War I. At dawn on April 9, more than 100,000 Canadian troops stormed up the ridge against heavy fire from artillery and machine guns. It took nearly four days of fighting to complete their victory, and in that time more than 10,000 Canadian men were killed or wounded. Vimy Ridge was an important position because it was higher than the surrounding country. This made it an important Allied position during the Hundred Days Offensive in 1918.

By the last days of the war, the Germans were forced to recruit boys as young as 16 to serve on the front line.

On the Western Front, German forces were almost back at the line where they had started their great offensive in March 1918. Within three weeks they had lost all the territory they had gained in the spring. Many German soldiers had also lost heart.

49

Crossing the Somme

5

By late August 1918, the Allies were slowly pushing east on a line that was 70 miles (112 km) long. Marshal Foch launched a series of three important attacks at different points in the line. His plan would feature Australian, Canadian, and other Allied forces that had already taken a major role in the fighting. It would also give the U.S. Army its first big chance in an independent action.

The target of the first attack was the French town of Peronne, then a German stronghold in the middle of the front line. It was on the side of the River Somme opposite the Allies' base. The battle would not be easy. The Germans had destroyed most of the bridges in the area, so the Allies would have to find new ways to cross the river.

Australian soldiers rested and posed for a picture before entering into battle.

The Australian commander, General John Monash, decided that the first step would be to take the nearby hill of Mont St. Quentin, which overlooked the town. His engineers built a new bridge over the Somme, and on August 30 the Australians crossed it. The attack began the next morning. The Australians charged up the slope against heavy gunfire, and within two hours they had captured the hill. A day later, the key town of Peronne was in Allied hands.

Foch's second target was the Hindenburg Line near the town of Arras. This stretch of the front line was another vital enemy stronghold, on the northern edge of the Hindenburg Line. Here the Germans had dug a deep trench system with concrete shelters, guarded by machine-gun posts and belts of barbed wire that were 100 yards (91 m) wide in places.

The assault began at dawn on September 2. First came the tanks. By now there were only 59 still working. The tanks were followed by Canadian troops. Once the Canadians had broken through the first line, British support units arrived. Within seven hours the Allies had captured this carefully built German defense system.

The next morning Canadian troops continued moving forward until they reached the high ground above the Canal du Nord. This waterway was wide and deep and would be difficult for troops to cross. German artillery and machine guns defended

it. The Canadians came under heavy fire and brought the advance to a halt. But since August 21, the Allies had moved about 15 miles (24 km) into German territory.

A group of Canadian soldiers moved into action by going over the top of a trench.

Foch's third target was the St. Mihiel salient. This was a large bulge in the German front line

53

near the city of Verdun. Besides being a threat to the town, the salient also blocked the railway to Paris and other important supply routes. Foch gave the task of capturing this area to Pershing and his U.S. forces, supported by the French. The U.S. Army was inexperienced and had played little part in the fighting. Now it had the chance to prove its power and efficiency.

Fighting was concentrated near the towns of Peronne, Arras, and Verdun.

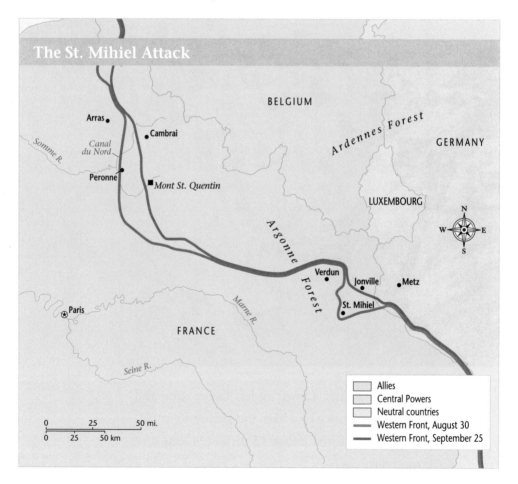

The St. Mihiel Attack

BELGIUM

GERMANY

LUXEMBOURG

Arras

Cambrai

Canal du Nord

Somme R.

Peronne

■ Mont St. Quentin

Ardennes Forest

Argonne Forest

Verdun

Jonville

Metz

St. Mihiel

Marne R.

Paris

FRANCE

Seine R.

| 0 | 25 | 50 mi. |
| 0 | 25 | 50 km |

Allies
Central Powers
Neutral countries
Western Front, August 30
Western Front, September 25

Pershing drew up detailed plans for every aspect of the assault. Under his command were 500,000 men, grouped in seven divisions. At that time, it was the largest American force that had ever gone into battle. Pershing also had newly trained units of tanks, led by the young Colonel George S. Patton.

French and British artillery began a heavy bombardment of the enemy defenses at 1 A.M. on September 12. Four hours later, part of the U.S. force of troops and tanks set off from the southeast side of the salient. At the same time, the rest of the force advanced from the northwest side. Their aim was to meet in the middle and cut off the territory inside the salient from the German front line. Meanwhile the French attacked the tip of the salient.

GEORGE S. PATTON

George S. Patton joined the U.S. Army in 1909. In 1912, he represented the United States in the pentathlon at the Olympic Games in Stockholm, Sweden. Sent to France in 1918, he commanded a tank brigade at St. Mihiel and was wounded by machine-gun fire. Patton became a legendary general in World War II, leading major offensives in North Africa, Sicily, France, and Germany.

Corporal Rudolph Forderhase was one of the first U.S. soldiers to go "over the top" in the battle. He described the experience:

> *The rain had made the clay muddy and slick. The shorter men had some difficulty getting out of the trench that was about four feet [1.2 m] deep. We formed squads to start across no-man's land. The enemy could not see us at first. When he did, we were greeted by machine-gun and rifle fire.*

55

In fact, the St. Mihiel attack turned out to be an easy operation. German commanders knew that an assault was coming and had withdrawn most of their men from the salient.

The German artillery was still retreating when the assault began. They left behind a few machine-gun posts to slow down the American advance. Even so, the attackers moved so quickly that they caught the last remaining defenders by surprise. In

American soldiers displayed a machine gun they had captured from the Germans in the St. Mihiel salient without firing a single shot.

some trenches, the Americans found food still on the tables and clothing scattered around, showing that the Germans had left in a hurry.

Pershing's tactics were an amazing success. He had ordered his commanders to lead their units from the front rather than staying behind like many other Allied officers. This encouraged the soldiers to advance quickly. The tank units under Patton had a huge impact. At one point, five tanks drove back

a large force of German infantry more than 6 miles (9.6 km) near the town of Jonville.

The St. Mihiel battle was also a landmark in air warfare. There were 180 U.S. planes on the Western Front in 1918. U.S. General Billy Mitchell commanded a force of nearly 1,500 British, French, and Italian planes during the action. It was the biggest air fleet ever assembled and the first time airpower had played an important part in a land battle.

Part of the air fleet kept a close watch on the movements of the German troops and flew air raids behind enemy lines. Another section of the air fleet attacked German observation balloons. The rest of the air fleet made a series of massive bombing raids behind enemy lines.

By the end of the next day, the two U.S. forces had joined up, making a continuous line across the salient. They had captured 16,000 prisoners and 450 guns but had suffered more than 7,000 casualties. It

AFRICAN-AMERICANS IN THE WAR

When the United States entered World War I, more than 350,000 African-Americans joined the Army. They were placed in two major units—each with white officers and segregated from white troops. The 92nd Infantry Division was mostly kept out of the fighting and perfomed jobs such as digging trenches. The 93rd Division was part of the U.S. Expeditionary Force to France. Its members trained with French soldiers and went into battle with them at St. Mihiel and the Argonne Forest. Many even wore French uniforms and used French weapons. The French government awarded 171 African-Americans the Croix de Guerre medal for bravery.

was the first big American success of the war and a boost to the soldiers' morale. It also proved to the rest of the Allies that the U.S. Army was a powerful fighting force. ◣

African-American soldiers from New York were among those who fought in the war.

Breaking the Hindenburg Line

Chapter

6

By late September 1918, the Allied forces had pinned the Germans back against the Hindenburg Line. The Western Front was now a long, curved line. In the north were the British, Australian, and Canadian troops, supported by the Belgians. In the center were the French, and in the south were the Americans. On the morning of September 26, they all lay waiting for the start of their biggest offensive yet—and they were all acting together. Opposite them, the Germans stood alone. Their main partner, Austria-Hungary, could not spare any troops from its struggle with Italy.

The U.S. units, with 600,000 men under General Pershing, were the first to move. After their smooth victory at St. Mihiel, they now had the chance to show how good they were in a major action. The attack started with a heavy bombardment by the artillery. American and French troops then attacked German positions on high ground near the vast Argonne Forest on the River Aisne.

Soldiers shielded their ears from the sound of a gun launching a shell into German territory in the Argonne Forest.

The U.S. soldiers advanced into battle against a blizzard of bullets. Sergeant William Triplet of the U.S. 35th Division noted how they tried to protect themselves:

It's odd how a man under fire will tilt his head forward and lean into his helmet like it was an umbrella in a hard rainstorm. It would take four helmet thicknesses to bounce a bullet. But it felt safer, peering from under the brim.

The first line of German defense fell quickly, but then there was strong resistance. The defenders brought in large numbers of reinforcements. Many Americans were going into battle for the first time. Moving through thick woodland was difficult for U.S. troops. They could not see far ahead and frequently got lost. It was also easy for defenders to fire on the attackers from hidden positions behind the trees.

Things grew worse the next day, September 27. It began to rain heavily, and the narrow roads to the front were thick with mud. Guns, supply wagons, and fresh units of soldiers found it difficult to get through. Heavy German gunfire slowed the American soldiers. Pershing was disappointed with the lack of progress, but he was forced to halt the attack.

On the same day, British and Canadian forces had pushed their way through the outer defenses of the Hindenburg Line. They were aiming to get to the

important town of Cambrai. After a battle with the Germans, the Canadians at last crossed the Canal du Nord, followed by the British. Then both groups fanned out into a line 6 miles (9.6 km) wide and fought their way forward. By evening, they were past the northern end of the Hindenburg Line.

Bombs and shell fire destroyed the landscape of the Argonne Forest as U.S. troops fought their way slowly forward.

63

The next phase of the Allied attacks began on September 28, just halfway into the 100 days. At the northern end of the Western Front, British and Belgian troops launched an attack near the town of Ypres. The Allied and German armies had been fighting over this area for four years. It was a wilderness of collapsed trenches, rusty barbed wire, burned-out tanks, and shell holes filled with water. Thousands of men had died here, too, and many of their corpses still lay under the mud. Now Allied soldiers took control of it in a single day, pushing the Germans back more than 5 miles (8 km).

The fourth part of the assault opened on September 29 to the south of Cambrai, where Allied soldiers faced a major obstacle that stood between them and the Hindenburg Line. It was the St. Quentin Canal. It had steep banks and deep water, and the Germans had destroyed nearly all of its bridges. It was impossible for tanks and other vehicles to cross over it. But there was a tunnel with a narrow path where the canal went underground.

THE BATTLE OF YPRES

The area near the French town of Ypres was one of the bloodiest battlegrounds of World War I. In 1914, British troops halted the huge German army invading France from the northeast. In 1915, the Germans attacked again, using poison gas on a large scale for the first time. In 1917, Ypres was the scene of the disastrous Allied attempt to capture the Passchendaele Ridge. German forces seized the area again during the March offensive in 1918 and were finally pushed out by the Allies. By the end of World War I, shells and bombs had destroyed the town of Ypres.

Allied artillery bombarded German fortifications for more than two days. In a huge barrage, the Allies hit the front of the Hindenburg Line with high-explosive shells and poison gas shells. German defenders took refuge in the deep canal tunnel.

At dawn, the American 27th and 30th divisions advanced toward the tunnel from two directions. On one side, the division immediately ran into the fire of enemy machine guns, which mowed down hundreds of American soldiers. The survivors had to take cover and could not move until evening. They had gained only a few yards.

Things seemed to go much better for the other division. By midmorning, the division had crossed through the tunnel, heading for the Hindenburg Line. But the soldiers were moving too quickly and did not wait for the Australian forces that were advancing to support them. German gunners came out of the tunnel where they had been hiding and began firing at the U.S. soldiers from behind, cutting them off from their own lines. Eventually the Australians arrived to help.

U.S. Private Willard M. Newton described the battleground a few hours later:

> *Scores of dead Americans, Australians, and Germans can be seen lying here and there, some covered with raincoats and others just lying as they fell. Walking wounded are going back in twos and threes, while those unable to walk are being carried off as rapidly as possible.*

65

Farther south, British forces had crossed the St. Quentin Canal by using rafts, small boats, and 3,000 life preservers. As they reached the eastern bank, a thick fog hid them from German gunners. British forces climbed the opposite slope of the canal and captured enemy positions. They even captured a vital bridge over the canal and stopped the Germans from destroying it.

British soldiers rested on the banks of the St. Quentin Canal after they had recaptured it.

From their new position, the British swept through a three-mile (4.8-km) stretch of the Hindenburg Line. They were able to link up with the struggling American and Australian troops to their left and help them move forward.

The assault at the St. Quentin Canal was the biggest success of the grand series of assaults all along the Western Front. Yet there was still no dramatic advance. The Germans continued to fight stubbornly, holding back the Allies. Rain, mud, and lack of supplies also slowed down the troops. The end of World War I was in sight, but no one knew how soon it would come. ◣

The Guns Fall Silent

7

Germany's military leaders gathered on September 28, 1918. They knew that they faced defeat. The German forces were in retreat all along the Western Front. The Austro-Hungarian army was about to surrender on the Italian border. Turkey had been badly beaten in the Middle East. The Central Powers were falling apart. On September 29 came the worst blow yet for the Central Powers—Bulgaria asked the Allies for a truce.

The stress and despair were too much for General Ludendorff. After months of overwork and worry, he had a seizure and fell to the floor, foaming at the mouth. Later he recovered enough to talk with von Hindenburg. The pair met Kaiser Wilhelm the next day and told him that Germany must find a way to end the war quickly—

General Erich Ludendorff (right) and Field Marshal Paul von Hindenburg commanded the German forces throughout the war.

they must approach U.S. President Woodrow Wilson to ask for a peace settlement. On October 4, the German government sent a message to Washington, D.C., asking the president to take steps for the restoration of peace.

While the Germans waited for a reply, the fighting continued. After the huge Allied advances of the last 60 days, it seemed victory was near. Yet most attacks had come to a standstill. In the north of France, deep mud and heavy rain slowed the movements of the Belgians and British. In the center of the Western Front, British and Australian troops were exhausted after their bloody breakthrough on the Hindenburg Line. And in the south, U.S. forces were picking their way slowly through the thick woodlands of the Argonne.

WILSON'S FOURTEEN POINTS

Why did the Germans ask the U.S. president, instead of the other Allied leaders, for a truce? It was because President Wilson had set out his own ideas for a lasting peace in Europe. On January 8, 1918, he had outlined the "Fourteen Points" to Congress. They included reducing the number of weapons in Europe, allowing freedom for all shipping on the seas, removing trade barriers, and withdrawing troops from invaded countries. The Germans believed Wilson's plan would give them the best terms for surrender. But Great Britain and France rejected some of the Fourteen Points and insisted that Germany should be given harsher terms. Wilson revised his own demands as the war dragged on.

During this time, heroic acts continued to take place. On October 8, a large unit of Germans in the woodlands ambushed a small American patrol. One man, Corporal Alvin York, refused to give up:

American soldiers rested after capturing the German second-line trenches in a section of the Argonne Forest.

There were over 30 of them, and all I could do was touch the Germans off just as fast as I could. I was sharp shooting. I don't think I missed a shot. It was no time to miss. All the time I kept yelling at them to come down. I didn't want to kill any more than I had to. But it was they or I. And I was giving them the best I had.

In the end, it was the Germans who surrendered. That day York killed 20 of them and captured 132 others. He was promoted to sergeant and was awarded the Medal of Honor, the highest U.S. military recognition.

The German army continued to retreat slowly. As the troops moved back toward the German border, they destroyed the landscape behind them. They blew up whole villages, tore out trees and crops, looted houses, and killed civilians as they went. This "scorched earth" policy was meant to make advancing more difficult for the Allies.

In fact, it probably delayed the end of the war. The German actions enraged Allied leaders, including President Wilson. They believed Germany could not be seriously asking for peace terms if its army was behaving in this way. There was more anger on October 10, when German submarines sank the Irish ship *Leinster* and drowned 520 passengers. Four days later, President Wilson refused the German request for a truce.

On October 23, Wilson sent his own demand to the German government. By this time he was taking a harder line than before. He and the Allied leaders now wanted not just an end to the war but also a complete German surrender. This would mean

THE GREAT INFLUENZA EPIDEMIC

Shells and bullets killed many men during 1918, but the outbreak of a deadly disease known as Spanish influenza killed even more. Nobody knows where the influenza outbreak started. Some scientists believe that U.S. troops from Kansas accidentally brought this deadly disease to the Western Front. That summer, vast numbers of troops on both sides died from the infection, which spread rapidly in the cramped and dirty conditions on the battlefield. By 1920, Spanish influenza had spread to most parts of the world. It killed at least 70 million people.

Germany would give up all its bargaining power. The demand shocked the people of Germany, and there were riots in many parts of the country.

Some American troops rode in French tanks to the battle line in the Argonne Forest.

Slowly, the Central Powers continued to crumble. Ludendorff resigned on October 26, and the German navy mutinied, refusing to obey orders. The Ottoman Empire signed an armistice on October 30, and Austria-Hungary did so three days later. Now Germany was on its own, and its armies were in full retreat.

Meanwhile, the fighting continued in the mud and rain of the Western Front. Soldiers on both sides were still being killed, wounded, or captured in vast numbers. During the entire Hundred Days, the U.S. Army alone suffered 127,000 casualties.

Private William Francis of the U.S. Marines recalled a bloody assault near the River Meuse on November 1:

> *We went over at 5:00 A.M. A shell went a few feet over my right shoulder and buried itself in the soft earth and only kicked mud over me. We had only gone about two hundred yards [182 m] when a machine gun opened up directly in front of us. It mowed the boys down. I finally spied the Germans in a trench. I kept firing and showed Arthur, who was on my right, where they were. Men all around us were being killed, Arthur and I being the only men alive in the front wave.*

At long last, on November 6, 1918, Germany asked the Allies for an armistice. Marshal Foch met the German leaders two days later in the forest of Compiègne in northern France. Foch called for a complete surrender and issued a list of Allied demands. The Germans had to withdraw from all occupied territory and give up all their weapons.

THE KAISER LEAVES HIS THRONE

The news of the armistice on November 8 sparked riots across Germany. Many of the demonstrators called on Kaiser Wilhelm to give up his throne. The German government also feared that the advancing Allies might capture him. The kaiser agreed to abdicate on November 9, and the next day he fled Germany. He spent the rest of his life in exile in the Netherlands—which had stayed neutral during the war—and died in 1941.

They had no choice but to agree. The Germans had to:

- Immediately abandon all occupied territory;
- Remove all troops from the West Bank of the River Rhine;
- Send home all Allied prisoners of war;
- Surrender all weapons, including submarines, artillery, aircraft, and battleships;
- Pay for the damage caused by the war.

But the war did not end immediately. Instead, Allied leaders fixed on a time three days ahead. They declared that the conflict would be officially over at exactly 11 A.M. on Monday, November 11—the 11th hour of the 11th day of the 11th month. This left a gap for the soldiers on the ground, who went on killing one another even though the result was certain.

News of the German surrender covered newspaper front pages around the world.

During the last three days of the Hundred Days Offensive, there was fierce fighting along parts of the Western Front. Many people on both sides believed they should carry on until the very last minute. Even on the morning of November 11, troops were still being sent into battle. At 10:50 A.M.—10 minutes before the ceasefire— British soldiers were ordered to capture an important river bridge at Lessines. Meanwhile, U.S. forces continued to battle through the Argonne.

On the German side, too, the guns kept firing. British Colonel W.N. Nicholson wrote:

> *A German machine gun remained in action the whole morning opposite our lines. Just before 11:00 A.M., 1,000 rounds were fired from it in a practically ceaseless burst. At five minutes to eleven the machine-gunner got up, took off his hat to us, and walked away.*

General Pershing was determined to keep U.S. troops moving forward and out of the Argonne. American guns went on pounding the German lines until the very last moment, too. But it came at last, as American Corporal Harry G. Wright recorded:

> *Now it is 11 o'clock November 11, 1918, and all our guns stopped and we stopped in our tracks and hugged each other and danced to keep warm and what a celebration was going on across the line on the Germans' side. They were shooting rockets and flares and hollering and dancing in glee.*

All along the Western Front the fighting stopped. Rifles, machine guns, and field guns ceased firing, and silence fell for the first time in four years. The Germans put down their weapons, and the Allied soldiers celebrated. The most terrible period of death and destruction the world had ever seen came to a sudden halt, and the threat of German domination of Europe vanished. World War I—and the Hundred Days Offensive—were over. ◼

On November 11, 1918, American soldiers celebrated when the fighting finally stopped.

The Legacy of the Hundred Days Offensive

Chapter

8

When the Battle of Amiens started the Hundred Days Offensive on the morning of August 8, 1918, World War I had already lasted 1,464 days, or more than four years. Both the Central Powers and the Allied armies were bogged down in their trenches, surrounded by a wilderness of mud, barbed wire, and shell craters. There seemed to be no way for either side to gain an advantage, break out of the deadlock, and make a major advance.

Yet within 100 days, Germany had surrendered and the Allies were celebrating a massive victory. This period brought the war to a surprisingly quick finish. Of course, no one knew at the time how long it would last. Only after the war ended did historians call this time the Hundred Days Offensive, although it lasted only 96 days.

Cheering crowds celebrated on the streets of New York City when the war officially ended.

There are many reasons that the Hundred Days Offensive proved to be so successful. First, the German army was exhausted by its efforts during the Kaiser's Battle of March 1918. Second, the arrival of forces from the United States in France brought fresh hope, as well as much-needed extra troops to the battered Allied side. Third, the Allied commanders used new tactics in their fighting. Instead of putting all their efforts into a single huge assault, they carefully planned a series of smaller attacks on different points along the enemy line. The development of better battle tanks made these attacks more effective.

In the end, the Hundred Days Offensive probably prevented several extra months of fighting. During this time, the old system of trench warfare and long-term attacks would have continued, and many thousands more soldiers would have been killed on both sides. It also ended the blockade of Germany, which had stopped food and other vital supplies from entering the country.

In addition, the Hundred Days Offensive turned the United States into a major military power. In 1914, the U.S. Army was small, with few modern weapons. Even when the United States entered the war in April 1917, it had just 100,000 trained troops. Yet by November 1918, the Army had grown to 4 million men, of which 2 million had been sent to fight overseas. In just a few short years, it had become the biggest national military force in the world.

American influence increased greatly during the Hundred Days Offensive. In 1914, President Wilson had insisted that his country should stay out of the fighting. He believed that by being neutral the United States could encourage both sides to agree to a ceasefire. When this policy failed, and the United States declared war on Germany, Wilson still planned for peace. In 1919, his Fourteen Points

CASUALTIES DURING THE HUNDRED DAYS OFFENSIVE

Total number of soldiers killed, wounded, or missing from August 8 to November 11, 1918

British Empire (Britain, Canada, New Zealand, and India)	411,600
France and North Africa	531,000
United States	127,000
Germany	785,700

Number of soldiers killed, wounded, or missing from 1914 to 1918 *

Key Allied Powers		Central Powers	
Australia	215,500	Austria-Hungary	4,650,200
Belgium	200,100	Bulgaria	346,900
France	1,853,400	Germany	7,209,400
Great Britain	2,555,800	Turkey	2,400,000
India	140,000		
Italy	2,197,000		
New Zealand	58,500		
Romania	535,700		
Russia	9,300,000		
Serbia	413,600		
United States	325,200		

* Numbers do not include total casualties during World War I

became the basis for the launch of the League of Nations, an international organization formed to prevent wars and the spread of weapons. It was replaced by the United Nations after World War II, in 1946.

After the war, a conference of world leaders was held from January 12 to 20, 1919, in Paris. Its aim was to discuss the future of the countries defeated in World War I and to plan for the future. The "Big Four" leaders of the main Allied

AMIENS. FRANCE 1919.

countries—France, Great Britain, the United States, and Italy—dominated the conference. They made sure that Germany and the other Central Powers were heavily punished for starting the war. Germany, for example, had to pay the cost of the damage caused by its part in the war, estimated at more than $13 billion.

The triumph of the Hundred Days Offensive could not disguise the terrible damage done by the war. The years of fighting had flattened cities,

Four years of war left almost every building in Amiens in ruins.

devastated vast areas of farmland, and destroyed empires. The war had left entire populations exhausted and economies wrecked. Above all, it had wiped out much of the younger generation of Great Britain, France, Germany, and other European countries, as well as in Australia, Canada, and India.

People in towns and villages throughout the world put up memorials with the names of those who had died. They mourned the loss of their

Stone crosses mark the graves of American soldiers who died fighting in the Argonne region in 1918.

84

loved ones. Many millions of soldiers who survived spent the rest of their lives handicapped by their wounds, both physical and mental. Soldiers with no physical wounds often had other problems when they arrived home, caused by the hardships and horrors they had suffered.

Even now, 90 years after the war ended, people in many countries of the world still remember those who suffered during the long conflict. On November 11 each year, special ceremonies are held in remembrance of the dead. In the United States, what began as Armistice Day is now Veterans Day, when Americans honor all veterans.

President Woodrow Wilson proclaimed November 11, 1919, as the first commemoration of Armistice Day. He said:

> *To us in America, the reflections of Armistice Day will be filled with solemn pride in the heroism of those who died in the country's service and with gratitude for the victory, both because of the thing from which it has freed us and because of the opportunity it has given America to show her sympathy with peace and justice in the councils of the nations.*

The United States, by standing side by side with its Allies in World War I, had forged a new position as a global power. It would forever alter the country's standing on the world stage. ◣

Timeline

June 28, 1914

Archduke Franz Ferdinand is assassinated in Sarajevo in Bosnia and Herzegovina.

July 28, 1914

Austria-Hungary declares war on Serbia.

August 1, 1914

Germany declares war on Russia.

August 3, 1914

Germany declares war on France.

August 4, 1914

German troops enter Belgium on their way to invade France; Great Britain declares war on Germany.

November 1914

The German advance is halted in northern France, and a deadlock begins on the Western Front.

May 7, 1915

German submarines sink a ship with American passengers aboard; U.S. public opinion in favor of the war hardens.

July 1, 1916

The Battle of the Somme begins.

January 19, 1917

U.S. President Woodrow Wilson has the text of the Zimmermann telegram, urging the Mexicans to side with Germany, published.

April 2, 1917

Wilson addresses the American people and promises war against Germany.

April 6, 1917

The United States declares war on Germany.

June 24, 1917

The first unit of U.S. troops lands in France.

January 8, 1918

Wilson publishes his Fourteen Points peace plan.

May 30, 1918

U.S. troops take part in their first major action in World War I.

August 8, 1918

The Hundred Days Offensive begins with the opening Allied attack and spectacular advance of the Battle of Amiens.

August 11, 1918

The Battle of Amiens ends.

August 21, 1918

The Allies attack the German-occupied towns of Albert and Bapaume.

August 31, 1918

Australian divisions capture Mont St. Quentin.

September 2, 1918

The Allied assault begins on the northern part of the Hindenburg Line near Arras.

September 12, 1918

U.S. and French troops begin their assault on the St. Mihiel salient.

September 13, 1918

The capture of the St. Mihiel salient is completed.

September 26, 1918

 A joint offensive by Allied forces at four points along the Western Front is launched.

September 28, 1918

The next phase begins halfway through the Hundred Days with the Allied attack near Ypres; German commanders meet at Spa, Germany, to discuss surrender terms.

September 29, 1918

Bulgaria agrees to surrender; the Allies advance on Cambrai; British, Australian, and U.S. troops cross the St. Quentin Canal.

October 4, 1918

The German government asks President Wilson to pass on a request for a peace settlement.

October 10, 1918

German submarines sink the Irish ship *Leinster*, killing 520 passengers.

October 14, 1918

Wilson rejects Germany's request.

October 23, 1918

Wilson demands a complete German surrender.

October 26, 1918

 General Ludendorff resigns as leader of the German army.

October 30, 1918

The Ottoman Empire officially surrenders.

November 2, 1918

Austria-Hungary officially surrenders, leaving Germany with no partners.

Timeline

November 6, 1918

Germany asks the Allies for
an armistice.

November 8, 1918

Allied and German leaders meet at
Compiègne to agree to peace terms.

November 11, 1918

World War I ends at 11 A.M.

January 12–20, 1919

The Paris Peace
Conference finalizes
treaties for the
defeated nations.

November 11, 1919

Wilson declares that Armistice Day
will be commemorated on this date
every year.

For more information on this topic, use FactHound.

1 Go to *www.facthound.com*

2 Type in this book ID: 0756538580

3 Click on the *Fetch It!* button.

FactHound will find the best Web sites for you.

HISTORIC SITES

National World War I Museum
100 W. 26th St.
Kansas City, MO 64108-4616
816/784-1918

The official World War I museum of the United States tells the story of those who served in World War I.

West Point Museum
U.S. Military Academy
West Point, NY 10996
914/938-2203

The museum contains a collection of U.S. military artifacts.

LOOK FOR MORE BOOKS IN THIS SERIES

Assassination in Sarajevo:
The Spark That Started World War I

The Berlin Airlift:
Breaking the Soviet Blockade

Black Tuesday:
Prelude to the Great Depression

Hiroshima and Nagasaki:
Fire From the Sky

Kristallnacht, The Night of Broken Glass:
Igniting the Nazi War Against Jews

Pearl Harbor:
Day of Infamy

A complete list of **Snapshots in History** titles is available on our Web site: *www.compasspointbooks.com*

Glossary

abdicate
step down

allies
friends or helpers; when capitalized, refers to the United States and its allies during World War I and World War II

armistice
formal agreement to end the fighting during a war

artillery
powerful weapons that fire rockets or shells

barrage
thick rain of shells on a limited area

blockade
military effort to keep goods from entering and leaving a region

bombardment
attack with bombs, shells, and other missiles

casualties
soldiers killed, captured, missing, or injured during a war

civilians
people not part of a military force

counterattack
attack in response to an attack by the enemy

division
large U.S. military group, made up of three regiments (or brigades) of soldiers; a division can include as many as 15,000 troops

field gun
large gun that can be moved around a battlefield

flame-thrower
weapon that shoots out a stream of lighted fuel

influenza
infectious disease that inflames the throat and causes fever

neutral
not taking part or giving assistance in a conflict

no-man's land
unoccupied area between opposing armies

offensive
attack

recruit
new member of the armed forces

reinforcements
extra units of soldiers used to support fighting troops

trench
long, narrow ditch dug by soldiers to protect them from gunfire

truce
short stop in fighting

Western Front
frontier between territory controlled by Germany and territory controlled by the Allies that was the main scene of fighting in World War I

Chapter 1

Page 9, line 9: "1918: Australians in France." 13 Feb. 2007. www.awm. gov.au/1918/feedback/memories_view.asp

Page 10, line 8: Ibid.

Page 11, line 6: Malcolm Brown. *The Imperial War Museum Book of the First World War*. Norman: University of Oklahoma Press, 1991, p. 86.

Page 15, line 7: Erich Ludendorff. *My War Memoirs 1914–1918*. London: Hutchinson, 1919, p. 674.

Chapter 2

Page 22, line 17: Edwin Campion Vaughan. *Some Desperate Glory: The Diary of a Young Officer, 1917*. London: Frederick Warne, 1981, p. 228.

Page 26, line 17: Hew Strachan. *The First World War*. London: Simon & Schuster, 2003, p. 221.

Chapter 3

Page 31, line 10: Peter Vansittart. *Voices from the Great War*. London: Jonathan Cape, 1981, p. 227.

Page 32, line 13: Richard van Emden. *Prisoners of the Kaiser: The Last POWs of the Great War*. Barnsley, South Yorkshire: Pen & Sword, 2000, p. 28.

Page 35, line 4: John Terraine. *The First World War 1914–18*. New York: Macmillan, 1965, p. 167.

Page 36, line 6: Vera Brittain. *Testament of Youth: An Autobiographical Study of the Years 1900–1925*. London: Gollancz, 1933, p. 420.

Chapter 4

Page 42, lines 2 and 4: J.H. Johnson. *1918: The Unexpected Victory*. New York: Sterling, 1997, p. 89.

Page 43, line 1: Ibid., p. 94.

Page 45, line 2: *The First World War 1914–18*, p. 176.

Page 48, line 6: *1918: The Unexpected Victory*, p. 123.

SOURCE NOTES

Chapter 5

Page 55, line 25: Martin Marix Evans. *Retreat, Hell! We Just Got Here! The American Expeditionary Force in France 1917–1918*. Oxford, England: Osprey Publishing, 1998, p. 63.

Chapter 6

Page 62, line 5: Ibid., p. 84.

Page 65, line 25: Joseph E. Persico. *11th Month, 11th Day, 11th Hour: Armistice Day 1918, World War I and Its Violent Climax*. New York: Random House, 2004, p. 285.

Chapter 7

Page 71, line 1: from *The Diary of Alvin C. York*. 13 Feb. 2007. http://acacia.pair.com/Acacia.Vignettes/The.Diary.of.Alvin.York.html

Page 74, line 4: *Retreat, Hell! We Just Got Here! The American Expeditionary Force in France 1917–1918*, p. 99.

Page 76, line 13: Lyn Macdonald. *1914–1918: Voices and Images of the Great War*. London: Penguin Books, 1988, p. 316.

Page 76, line 24: *Retreat, Hell! We Just Got Here! The American Expeditionary Force in France 1917–1918*, p. 108.

Chapter 8

Page 85, line 18: "History of Veterans Day." United States Department of Veterans Affairs. 3 Nov. 2007. www1.va.gov/opa/vetsday/vetdayhistory.asp

SELECT BIBLIOGRAPHY

Brown, Malcolm. *The Imperial War Museum Book of the First World War.* Norman: University of Oklahoma Press, 1991.

Johnson, J.H. *1918: The Unexpected Victory.* New York: Sterling, 1997.

Macdonald, Lyn. *1914–1918: Voices and Images of the Great War.* London: Penguin Books, 1988.

Persico, Joseph E. *11th Month, 11th Day, 11th Hour: Armistice Day 1918, World War I and Its Violent Climax.* New York: Random House, 2004.

Pitt, Barrie. *1918: The Last Act.* London: Cassell, 1962.

Strachan, Hew. *The First World War.* London: Simon & Schuster, 2003.

Terraine, John. *The First World War 1914–18.* New York: Macmillan, 1965.

Van Emden, Richard. *Prisoners of the Kaiser: The Last POWs of the Great War.* Barnsley, South Yorkshire: Pen & Sword, 2000.

FURTHER READING

Adams, Simon. *Causes and Consequences.* New York: Franklin Watts, 2004.

Coetzee, Frans, and Marilyn Shevin-Coetzee. *World War I: A History in Documents.* New York: Oxford University Press, 2002.

Dowswell, Paul. *The Western Front in World War I.* London: Hodder Wayland, 2004.

Feldman, Ruth Tenzer. *World War I.* Minneapolis: Lerner Publications Company, 2004.

Gilbert, Adrian. *Going to War in World War I.* New York: Franklin Watts, 2001.

Worth, Richard. *America in World War I.* Milwaukee: World Almanac Library, 2007.

Index

ABOUT THE AUTHOR

Andrew Langley is the author of many history books for children. These include a biography of Mikhail Gorbachev, *The Roman News*, and *A Castle at War*, which was shortlisted for the *Times* Education Supplement Information Book Award. He lives in England, with his family and two dogs.

IMAGE CREDITS